I0202864

Join Our Team
Achieve a Dream
Knowledge Changes You
You Change the World

SMART ⒶGRADES
NEXT EVOLUTION BRAIN POWER REVOLUTION

What's Inside?

✔ Academic Calendar

✔ Take Great Class Notes

✔ Active Listening Skills

✔ Write Daily Test Review Notes

✔ Use Association Cues for Instant and Total Recall

✔ Convert Facts into Test Questions

✔ Review for Retention, Recognition, and Recall

✔ Self-Test for Instant and Total Recall

✔ Power Study Snacks

WE ARE THE FUTURE
EVERYBODY IS SOMEBODY SPECIAL

Academic Calendar: August-January

August

Class	What's Due?	Due Date

Back to School: Get Organized, Prepare Study Room, Purchase School Supplies

----

September

_____

October

November

December

January

Academic Calendar: February-June

February Class	What's Due?	Due Date
--------------------	--------------------	--------------------
--------------------	--------------------	--------------------
--------------------	--------------------	--------------------

March

--------------------	--------------------	--------------------
--------------------	--------------------	--------------------
--------------------	--------------------	--------------------

April

--------------------	--------------------	--------------------
--------------------	--------------------	--------------------
--------------------	--------------------	--------------------

May

--------------------	--------------------	--------------------
--------------------	--------------------	--------------------
--------------------	--------------------	--------------------

June

--------------------	--------------------	--------------------
--------------------	--------------------	--------------------
--------------------	--------------------	--------------------

@2000. All Rights Reserved. **SMARTGRADES INC.**

He who asks a question may be a fool for five minutes,
but he who never asks a question remains a fool forever.

Tom J. Connelly

SMARTGRADES:NEXT EVOLUTION BRAIN POWER REVOLUTION

My Class Schedule (fixed)
Class:
Teacher:
Day(s):
Time:

My Regular Study Schedule (variable)
Quiet Study Space:
Day(s):
Time:
My Favorite Power Study Snack to Stay Energized and Focused (see list):

My Teacher's Office Hours
Office Address:
Phone #:
E-mail:
Day(s):
Time:

Nine Good Reasons to Visit Your Teacher:
1. Introduce yourself
2. Seek clarification of academic material
3. Ask for approval of your topic and outline
4. Seek constructive criticism of your rough draft
5. To complain about an unfair test question
6. To correct a grading error
7. You will be absent from class due to a private matter
8. Ask for a recommendation for a job/school
9. Express gratitude for a great class

My School's Tutoring Center
Address:
Phone:
E-mail:
Day(s):
Time:
Tutor's Name and E-mail:

My Study Buddies Contact Information

Classmate:
Phone #:
E-mail:

Classmate:
Phone #:
E-mail:

Classmate:
Phone #:
E-mail:

Superhighway of Academic Success

The Academic Facts Move from a Blackboard, to a Notebook, to a Homework Assignment, Through Your Powerful Brain, and to a Test

Learn to Listen and Listen to Learn

SMARTGRADES In-Class Active Listening Skills

1. Pre-read the lecture topic. ✔

2. Clear your mind of all distractions (thoughts, feelings: worry, anxiety, and fear). ✔

3. Focus. Follow the speaker's line of argument. ✔

4. Selectively listen for the key facts, phrases, and words. ✔

5. What does the speaker focus on? Concepts? Formulas? ✔

6. As questions arise, write them down in the margins of your notebook. ✔

7. Ask your teacher for clarification. ✔

8. Do not leave class feeling lost, confused, or hopeless. ✔

Plan Your Work and Work Your Plan

SMARTGRADES In-Class Note Taking Skills

1. Take organized notes: Write down the main ideas and supporting details. ✔

2. To write quickly, use abbreviations and shorthand symbols. ✔

3. Bring extra pens and pencils. ✔

4. Write the homework assignment down in a SMARTGRADES Academic Assignment Planner (not in your head) and double check it for accuracy. ✔

Failing to Prepare Is Preparing to Fail

SMARTGRADES After-Class Test Review Notes to Ace Your Test

1. Choose a study area that is free of external and social distractions: _____ ✔

2. Eat a **Power Study Snack** to stay energized and focused (see list): _____ ✔

3. **Manage your time.** ✔
Estimate Time (Fantasy):   Start Time: Finish Time: **Actual Time (Reality):**

4. After every class, read your class notes and underline/highlight the <u>main ideas</u> and <u>supporting details.</u> ✔

5. **Condensation** (Distillation): Outline/summarize your class notes into **Test Review Notes.** ✔

6. Do the facts need further clarification (see another textbook, tutoring center, or teacher)? ✔

7. Visualize the test question. Convert the facts into a test question: Define Terms? Compare? Contrast? Cause and Effect? Pros and Cons? List? Prove? Discuss? Outline? Agree or Disagree? ✔

8. Use **Association Cues** to memorize facts for **Instant and Total Recall.** Attach an unknown fact to a known fact stored in your memory. Use very personal memories for higher rates of retention. ✔

Acrostic Cue: Use a sentence to condense the key facts. For example, to remember the order of G-clef notes on sheet music, (E, G, B, D, F,) use the classic acrostic: Every Good Boy Deserves Fun.

Rhyme Cue: Use rhymes to link the key facts together. For example, the classic,"I before E, except after C."

Music Cue: Make up a song or poem with the information in it. Sing the song or recite the poem several times.

Chaining Cue: Create a story where each word or idea you have to remember cues the next idea you need to recall. Use your imagination. If you had to remember the name, Shirley Temple, you could rhyme Shirley with curly and remember that she had curly hair around her temples.

Funny Cue: Write a joke that contains the key facts. The funniest, most outlandish, and the strangest concoction of memory cues makes memorizing easy.

9. Two weeks before the test, **Self-Test** for strengths and weaknesses (change weak cues). ✔

10. The day of the test, review your study notes to refresh your memory. Ace the Test. ✔

Take Control of Your Day, Your Dream and Your Destiny!

My Class Notes   Date:

Topic:

Write down the <u>Main Idea</u> and the supporting <u>Details</u>, <u>Examples</u>, or <u>Arguments</u>:

_____
_____
_____
_____
_____
_____
_____
_____
_____
_____
_____
_____
_____
_____
_____
_____
_____
_____
_____
_____
_____
_____
_____
_____
_____
_____
_____
_____
_____
_____
_____
_____
_____
_____

My Class Notes Continued . . .

My Class Notes Continued . . .

Part 1. After Class, Write Test-Review Notes: Association Cues

1. Right after class, read your class notes, and condense them into Test Review Notes ✔
2. Choose a study area that is free of external and social distractions ✔
3. Eat a Power Study Snack to stay energized and focused (see list) ✔
4. Manage your time ✔

    Estimate Time (Fantasy):   Start Time: Finish Time: Actual Time (Reality):

5. Do the facts need further clarification (see textbook, tutoring center, or teacher)? ✔
6. To ace your test, use Association Cues to memorize the facts for Instant and Total Recall ✔

Write Memory Association Cues for Instant and Total Recall
(Use pencil to change a cue that doesn't work)

Part 2. After Class, Write Test Review Notes: Create Test Questions

7. Visualize the test questions. Convert the facts into test questions: Who? Why? Where? What? ✔

8. Self-Test for strengths and weaknesses. Change the weak memory cues ✔

9. To ace your test: Review, Repetition, Retention, Recognition, and Instant and Total Recall ✔

Write Test Questions: Who, What? Where? When? Why?

My Class Notes

Date:

Topic:

Write down the <u>Main Idea</u> and the supporting <u>Details</u>, <u>Examples</u>, or <u>Arguments</u>:

_____
_____
_____
_____
_____
_____
_____
_____
_____
_____
_____
_____
_____
_____
_____
_____
_____
_____
_____
_____
_____
_____
_____
_____
_____
_____
_____
_____
_____
_____
_____
_____

My Class Notes Continued . . .

Part 1. After Class, Write Test-Review Notes: Association Cues

1. Right after class, read your class notes, and condense them into Test Review Notes ✔
2. Choose a study area that is free of external and social distractions ✔
3. Eat a Power Study Snack to stay energized and focused (see list) ✔
4. Manage your time ✔

   Estimate Time (Fantasy):   Start Time: Finish Time: Actual Time (Reality):

5. Do the facts need further clarification (see textbook, tutoring center, or teacher)? ✔
6. To ace your test, use Association Cues to memorize the facts for Instant and Total Recall ✔

Write Memory Association Cues for Instant and Total Recall
(Use pencil to change a cue that doesn't work)

Part 2. After Class, Write Test Review Notes: Create Test Questions

7. Visualize the test questions. Convert the facts into test questions: Who? Why? Where? What? ✔

8. Self-Test for strengths and weaknesses. Change the weak memory cues ✔

9. To ace your test: Review, Repetition, Retention, Recognition, and Instant and Total Recall ✔

Write Test Questions: Who, What? Where? When? Why?

My Class Notes

Date:

Topic:

Write down the <u>Main Idea</u> and the supporting <u>Details</u>, <u>Examples</u>, or <u>Arguments</u>:

_____
_____
_____
_____
_____
_____
_____
_____
_____
_____
_____
_____
_____
_____
_____
_____
_____
_____
_____
_____
_____
_____
_____
_____
_____
_____
_____
_____
_____
_____
_____
_____
_____
_____
_____

My Class Notes Continued . . .

My Class Notes Continued . . .

Part 1. After Class, Write Test-Review Notes: Association Cues

1. Right after class, read your class notes, and condense them into Test Review Notes ✔
2. Choose a study area that is free of external and social distractions ✔
3. Eat a Power Study Snack to stay energized and focused (see list) ✔
4. Manage your time ✔

   Estimate Time (Fantasy):   Start Time: Finish Time: Actual Time (Reality):

5. Do the facts need further clarification (see textbook, tutoring center, or teacher)? ✔
6. To ace your test, use Association Cues to memorize the facts for Instant and Total Recall ✔

Write Memory Association Cues for Instant and Total Recall
(Use pencil to change a cue that doesn't work)

Part 2. After Class, Write Test Review Notes: Create Test Questions

7. Visualize the test questions. Convert the facts into test questions: Who? Why? Where? What? ✔

8. Self-Test for strengths and weaknesses. Change the weak memory cues ✔

9. To ace your test: Review, Repetition, Retention, Recognition, and Instant and Total Recall ✔

Write Test Questions: Who, What? Where? When? Why?

My Class Notes   Date:

Topic:

Write down the <u>Main Idea</u> and the supporting <u>Details</u>, <u>Examples</u>, or <u>Arguments</u>:

_____
_____
_____
_____
_____
_____
_____
_____
_____
_____
_____
_____
_____
_____
_____
_____
_____
_____
_____
_____
_____
_____
_____
_____
_____
_____
_____
_____
_____
_____
_____
_____
_____
_____

My Class Notes Continued . . .

My Class Notes Continued . . .

Part 1. After Class, Write Test-Review Notes: Association Cues

1. Right after class, read your class notes, and condense them into Test Review Notes ✔

2. Choose a study area that is free of external and social distractions ✔

3. Eat a Power Study Snack to stay energized and focused (see list) ✔

4. Manage your time ✔

    Estimate Time (Fantasy):   Start Time: Finish Time: Actual Time (Reality):

5. Do the facts need further clarification (see textbook, tutoring center, or teacher)? ✔

6. To ace your test, use Association Cues to memorize the facts for Instant and Total Recall ✔

Write Memory Association Cues for Instant and Total Recall
(Use pencil to change a cue that doesn't work)

Part 2. After Class, Write Test Review Notes: Create Test Questions

7. Visualize the test questions. Convert the facts into test questions: Who? Why? Where? What? ✔

8. Self-Test for strengths and weaknesses. Change the weak memory cues ✔

9. To ace your test: Review, Repetition, Retention, Recognition, and Instant and Total Recall ✔

Write Test Questions: Who, What? Where? When? Why?

My Class Notes   Date:

Topic:

Write down the <u>Main Idea</u> and the supporting <u>Details</u>, <u>Examples</u>, or <u>Arguments</u>:

_____
_____
_____
_____
_____
_____
_____
_____
_____
_____
_____
_____
_____
_____
_____
_____
_____
_____
_____
_____
_____
_____
_____
_____
_____
_____
_____
_____
_____
_____
_____
_____
_____
_____

My Class Notes Continued . . .

Part 1. After Class, Write Test-Review Notes: Association Cues

1. Right after class, read your class notes, and condense them into Test Review Notes ✔

2. Choose a study area that is free of external and social distractions ✔

3. Eat a Power Study Snack to stay energized and focused (see list) ✔

4. Manage your time ✔

    Estimate Time (Fantasy):   Start Time: Finish Time: Actual Time (Reality):

5. Do the facts need further clarification (see textbook, tutoring center, or teacher)? ✔

6. To ace your test, use Association Cues to memorize the facts for Instant and Total Recall ✔

Write Memory Association Cues for Instant and Total Recall
(Use pencil to change a cue that doesn't work)

Part 2. After Class, Write Test Review Notes: Create Test Questions

7. Visualize the test questions. Convert the facts into test questions: Who? Why? Where? What? ✔

8. Self-Test for strengths and weaknesses. Change the weak memory cues ✔

9. To ace your test: Review, Repetition, Retention, Recognition, and Instant and Total Recall ✔

Write Test Questions: Who, What? Where? When? Why?

My Class Notes   Date:

Topic:

Write down the <u>Main Idea</u> and the supporting <u>Details</u>, <u>Examples</u>, or <u>Arguments</u>:

_____
_____
_____
_____
_____
_____
_____
_____
_____
_____
_____
_____
_____
_____
_____
_____
_____
_____
_____
_____
_____
_____
_____
_____
_____
_____
_____
_____
_____
_____
_____

My Class Notes   Date:

Topic:

Write down the <u>Main Idea</u> and the supporting <u>Details</u>, <u>Examples</u>, or <u>Arguments</u>:

Part 1. After Class, Write Test-Review Notes: Association Cues

1. Right after class, read your class notes, and condense them into Test Review Notes ✔
2. Choose a study area that is free of external and social distractions ✔
3. Eat a Power Study Snack to stay energized and focused (see list) ✔
4. Manage your time ✔

   Estimate Time (Fantasy):   Start Time: Finish Time: Actual Time (Reality):

5. Do the facts need further clarification (see textbook, tutoring center, or teacher)? ✔
6. To ace your test, use Association Cues to memorize the facts for Instant and Total Recall ✔

Write Memory Association Cues for Instant and Total Recall
(Use pencil to change a cue that doesn't work)

Part 2. After Class, Write Test Review Notes: Create Test Questions

7. Visualize the test questions. Convert the facts into test questions: Who? Why? Where? What? ✔

8. Self-Test for strengths and weaknesses. Change the weak memory cues ✔

9. To ace your test: Review, Repetition, Retention, Recognition, and Instant and Total Recall ✔

Write Test Questions: Who, What? Where? When? Why?

My Class Notes

Date:

Topic:

Write down the <u>Main Idea</u> and the supporting <u>Details</u>, <u>Examples</u>, or <u>Arguments</u>:

_____
_____
_____
_____
_____
_____
_____
_____
_____
_____
_____
_____
_____
_____
_____
_____
_____
_____
_____
_____
_____
_____
_____
_____
_____
_____
_____
_____
_____
_____
_____
_____

My Class Notes Continued . . .

Part 1. After Class, Write Test-Review Notes: Association Cues

1. Right after class, read your class notes, and condense them into Test Review Notes ✔

2. Choose a study area that is free of external and social distractions ✔

3. Eat a Power Study Snack to stay energized and focused (see list) ✔

4. Manage your time ✔

   Estimate Time (Fantasy):   Start Time: Finish Time: Actual Time (Reality):

5. Do the facts need further clarification (see textbook, tutoring center, or teacher)? ✔

6. To ace your test, use Association Cues to memorize the facts for Instant and Total Recall ✔

Write Memory Association Cues for Instant and Total Recall
(Use pencil to change a cue that doesn't work)

Part 2. After Class, Write Test Review Notes: Create Test Questions

7. Visualize the test questions. Convert the facts into test questions: Who? Why? Where? What? ✔

8. Self-Test for strengths and weaknesses. Change the weak memory cues ✔

9. To ace your test: Review, Repetition, Retention, Recognition, and Instant and Total Recall ✔

Write Test Questions: Who, What? Where? When? Why?

My Class Notes

Date:

Topic:

Write down the <u>Main Idea</u> and the supporting <u>Details</u>, <u>Examples</u>, or <u>Arguments</u>:

_____
_____
_____
_____
_____
_____
_____
_____
_____
_____
_____
_____
_____
_____
_____
_____
_____
_____
_____
_____
_____
_____
_____
_____
_____
_____
_____
_____
_____
_____
_____
_____
_____
_____
_____
_____

My Class Notes Continued . . .

Part 1. After Class, Write Test-Review Notes: Association Cues

1. Right after class, read your class notes, and condense them into Test Review Notes ✔

2. Choose a study area that is free of external and social distractions ✔

3. Eat a Power Study Snack to stay energized and focused (see list) ✔

4. Manage your time ✔

    Estimate Time (Fantasy):   Start Time: Finish Time: Actual Time (Reality):

5. Do the facts need further clarification (see textbook, tutoring center, or teacher)? ✔

6. To ace your test, use Association Cues to memorize the facts for Instant and Total Recall ✔

Write Memory Association Cues for Instant and Total Recall
(Use pencil to change a cue that doesn't work)

Part 2. After Class, Write Test Review Notes: Create Test Questions

7. Visualize the test questions. Convert the facts into test questions: Who? Why? Where? What? ✔

8. Self-Test for strengths and weaknesses. Change the weak memory cues ✔

9. To ace your test: Review, Repetition, Retention, Recognition, and Instant and Total Recall ✔

Write Test Questions: Who, What? Where? When? Why?

My Class Notes   Date:

Topic:

Write down the <u>Main Idea</u> and the supporting <u>Details</u>, <u>Examples</u>, or <u>Arguments</u>:

_____

_____

_____

_____

_____

_____

_____

_____

_____

_____

_____

_____

_____

_____

_____

_____

_____

_____

_____

_____

_____

_____

_____

_____

_____

_____

_____

_____

_____

_____

_____

Part 1. After Class, Write Test-Review Notes: Association Cues

1. Right after class, read your class notes, and condense them into Test Review Notes ✔
2. Choose a study area that is free of external and social distractions ✔
3. Eat a Power Study Snack to stay energized and focused (see list) ✔
4. Manage your time ✔

   Estimate Time (Fantasy):   Start Time: Finish Time: Actual Time (Reality):

5. Do the facts need further clarification (see textbook, tutoring center, or teacher)? ✔
6. To ace your test, use Association Cues to memorize the facts for Instant and Total Recall ✔

Write Memory Association Cues for Instant and Total Recall
(Use pencil to change a cue that doesn't work)

Part 2. After Class, Write Test Review Notes: Create Test Questions

7. Visualize the test questions. Convert the facts into test questions: Who? Why? Where? What? ✔

8. Self-Test for strengths and weaknesses. Change the weak memory cues ✔

9. To ace your test: Review, Repetition, Retention, Recognition, and Instant and Total Recall ✔

Write Test Questions: Who, What? Where? When? Why?

My Class Notes   **Date:**

Topic:

Write down the <u>Main Idea</u> and the supporting <u>Details</u>, <u>Examples</u>, or <u>Arguments</u>:

_____
_____
_____
_____
_____
_____
_____
_____
_____
_____
_____
_____
_____
_____
_____
_____
_____
_____
_____
_____
_____
_____
_____
_____
_____
_____
_____
_____
_____
_____
_____
_____
_____
_____

Part 1. After Class, Write Test-Review Notes: Association Cues

1. Right after class, read your class notes, and condense them into Test Review Notes ✔
2. Choose a study area that is free of external and social distractions ✔
3. Eat a Power Study Snack to stay energized and focused (see list) ✔
4. Manage your time ✔

   Estimate Time (Fantasy):   Start Time: Finish Time: Actual Time (Reality):

5. Do the facts need further clarification (see textbook, tutoring center, or teacher)? ✔
6. To ace your test, use Association Cues to memorize the facts for Instant and Total Recall ✔

Write Memory Association Cues for Instant and Total Recall
(Use pencil to change a cue that doesn't work)

Part 2. After Class, Write Test Review Notes: Create Test Questions

7. Visualize the test questions. Convert the facts into test questions: Who? Why? Where? What? ✔

8. Self-Test for strengths and weaknesses. Change the weak memory cues ✔

9. To ace your test: Review, Repetition, Retention, Recognition, and Instant and Total Recall ✔

Write Test Questions: Who, What? Where? When? Why?

My Class Notes

Date:

Topic:

Write down the <u>Main Idea</u> and the supporting <u>Details</u>, <u>Examples</u>, or <u>Arguments</u>:

My Class Notes Continued . . .

Part 1. After Class, Write Test-Review Notes: Association Cues

1. Right after class, read your class notes, and condense them into Test Review Notes ✔

2. Choose a study area that is free of external and social distractions ✔

3. Eat a Power Study Snack to stay energized and focused (see list) ✔

4. Manage your time ✔

   Estimate Time (Fantasy):   Start Time: Finish Time: Actual Time (Reality):

5. Do the facts need further clarification (see textbook, tutoring center, or teacher)? ✔

6. To ace your test, use Association Cues to memorize the facts for Instant and Total Recall ✔

Write Memory Association Cues for Instant and Total Recall
(Use pencil to change a cue that doesn't work)

Part 2. After Class, Write Test Review Notes: Create Test Questions

7. Visualize the test questions. Convert the facts into test questions: Who? Why? Where? What? ✔

8. Self-Test for strengths and weaknesses. Change the weak memory cues ✔

9. To ace your test: Review, Repetition, Retention, Recognition, and Instant and Total Recall ✔

Write Test Questions: Who, What? Where? When? Why?

My Class Notes   Date:

Topic:

Write down the <u>Main Idea</u> and the supporting <u>Details</u>, <u>Examples</u>, or <u>Arguments</u>:

_____
_____
_____
_____
_____
_____
_____
_____
_____
_____
_____
_____
_____
_____
_____
_____
_____
_____
_____
_____
_____
_____
_____
_____
_____
_____
_____
_____
_____
_____
_____
_____

My Class Notes Continued . . .

Part 1. After Class, Write Test-Review Notes: Association Cues

1. Right after class, read your class notes, and condense them into Test Review Notes ✔
2. Choose a study area that is free of external and social distractions ✔
3. Eat a Power Study Snack to stay energized and focused (see list) ✔
4. Manage your time ✔

   Estimate Time (Fantasy):   Start Time: Finish Time: Actual Time (Reality):

5. Do the facts need further clarification (see textbook, tutoring center, or teacher)? ✔
6. To ace your test, use Association Cues to memorize the facts for Instant and Total Recall ✔

Write Memory Association Cues for Instant and Total Recall
(Use pencil to change a cue that doesn't work)

Part 2. After Class, Write Test Review Notes: Create Test Questions

7. Visualize the test questions. Convert the facts into test questions: Who? Why? Where? What? ✔

8. Self-Test for strengths and weaknesses. Change the weak memory cues ✔

9. To ace your test: Review, Repetition, Retention, Recognition, and Instant and Total Recall ✔

Write Test Questions: Who, What? Where? When? Why?

My Class Notes

Date:

Topic:

Write down the <u>Main Idea</u> and the supporting <u>Details</u>, <u>Examples</u>, or <u>Arguments</u>:

_____
_____
_____
_____
_____
_____
_____
_____
_____
_____
_____
_____
_____
_____
_____
_____
_____
_____
_____
_____
_____
_____
_____
_____
_____
_____
_____
_____
_____
_____
_____
_____
_____
_____
_____

My Class Notes Continued . . .

Part 1. After Class, Write Test-Review Notes: Association Cues

1. Right after class, read your class notes, and condense them into Test Review Notes ✔

2. Choose a study area that is free of external and social distractions ✔

3. Eat a Power Study Snack to stay energized and focused (see list) ✔

4. Manage your time ✔

   Estimate Time (Fantasy):   Start Time: Finish Time: Actual Time (Reality):

5. Do the facts need further clarification (see textbook, tutoring center, or teacher)? ✔

6. To ace your test, use Association Cues to memorize the facts for Instant and Total Recall ✔

Write Memory Association Cues for Instant and Total Recall
(Use pencil to change a cue that doesn't work)

Part 2. After Class, Write Test Review Notes: Create Test Questions

7. Visualize the test questions. Convert the facts into test questions: Who? Why? Where? What? ✔

8. Self-Test for strengths and weaknesses. Change the weak memory cues ✔

9. To ace your test: Review, Repetition, Retention, Recognition, and Instant and Total Recall ✔

Write Test Questions: Who, What? Where? When? Why?

My Class Notes   Date:

Topic:

Write down the <u>Main Idea</u> and the supporting <u>Details</u>, <u>Examples</u>, or <u>Arguments</u>:

_____

_____

_____

_____

_____

_____

_____

_____

_____

_____

_____

_____

_____

_____

_____

_____

_____

_____

_____

_____

_____

_____

_____

_____

_____

_____

_____

_____

_____

_____

_____

_____

Part 1. After Class, Write Test-Review Notes: Association Cues

1. Right after class, read your class notes, and condense them into Test Review Notes ✔

2. Choose a study area that is free of external and social distractions ✔

3. Eat a Power Study Snack to stay energized and focused (see list) ✔

4. Manage your time ✔

    Estimate Time (Fantasy):   Start Time: Finish Time: Actual Time (Reality):

5. Do the facts need further clarification (see textbook, tutoring center, or teacher)? ✔

6. To ace your test, use Association Cues to memorize the facts for Instant and Total Recall ✔

Write Memory Association Cues for Instant and Total Recall
(Use pencil to change a cue that doesn't work)

Part 2. After Class, Write Test Review Notes: Create Test Questions

7. Visualize the test questions. Convert the facts into test questions: Who? Why? Where? What? ✔

8. Self-Test for strengths and weaknesses. Change the weak memory cues ✔

9. To ace your test: Review, Repetition, Retention, Recognition, and Instant and Total Recall ✔

Write Test Questions: Who, What? Where? When? Why?

My Class Notes   Date:

Topic:

Write down the <u>Main Idea</u> and the supporting <u>Details</u>, <u>Examples</u>, or <u>Arguments</u>:

_____

_____

_____

_____

_____

_____

_____

_____

_____

_____

_____

_____

_____

_____

_____

_____

_____

_____

_____

_____

_____

_____

_____

_____

_____

_____

_____

_____

_____

_____

_____

_____

Part 1. After Class, Write Test-Review Notes: Association Cues

1. Right after class, read your class notes, and condense them into Test Review Notes ✔

2. Choose a study area that is free of external and social distractions ✔

3. Eat a Power Study Snack to stay energized and focused (see list) ✔

4. Manage your time ✔

    Estimate Time (Fantasy):   Start Time: Finish Time: Actual Time (Reality):

5. Do the facts need further clarification (see textbook, tutoring center, or teacher)? ✔

6. To ace your test, use Association Cues to memorize the facts for Instant and Total Recall ✔

Write Memory Association Cues for Instant and Total Recall
(Use pencil to change a cue that doesn't work)

Part 2. After Class, Write Test Review Notes: Create Test Questions

7. Visualize the test questions. Convert the facts into test questions: Who? Why? Where? What? ✔

8. Self-Test for strengths and weaknesses. Change the weak memory cues ✔

9. To ace your test: Review, Repetition, Retention, Recognition, and Instant and Total Recall ✔

Write Test Questions: Who, What? Where? When? Why?

My Class Notes

Date:

Topic:

Write down the <u>Main Idea</u> and the supporting <u>Details</u>, <u>Examples</u>, or <u>Arguments</u>:

_____

_____

_____

_____

_____

_____

_____

_____

_____

_____

_____

_____

_____

_____

_____

_____

_____

_____

_____

_____

_____

_____

_____

_____

_____

_____

_____

_____

_____

_____

_____

_____

My Class Notes Continued . . .

Part 1. After Class, Write Test-Review Notes: Association Cues

1. Right after class, read your class notes, and condense them into Test Review Notes ✔

2. Choose a study area that is free of external and social distractions ✔

3. Eat a Power Study Snack to stay energized and focused (see list) ✔

4. Manage your time ✔

   Estimate Time (Fantasy):   Start Time: Finish Time: Actual Time (Reality):

5. Do the facts need further clarification (see textbook, tutoring center, or teacher)? ✔

6. To ace your test, use Association Cues to memorize the facts for Instant and Total Recall ✔

Write Memory Association Cues for Instant and Total Recall
(Use pencil to change a cue that doesn't work)

Part 2. After Class, Write Test Review Notes: Create Test Questions

7. Visualize the test questions. Convert the facts into test questions: Who? Why? Where? What? ✔

8. Self-Test for strengths and weaknesses. Change the weak memory cues ✔

9. To ace your test: Review, Repetition, Retention, Recognition, and Instant and Total Recall ✔

Write Test Questions: Who, What? Where? When? Why?

My Class Notes   **Date:**

Topic:

Write down the <u>Main Idea</u> and the supporting <u>Details</u>, <u>Examples</u>, or <u>Arguments</u>:

_____

_____

_____

_____

_____

_____

_____

_____

_____

_____

_____

_____

_____

_____

_____

_____

_____

_____

_____

_____

_____

_____

_____

_____

_____

_____

_____

_____

_____

_____

_____

_____

Part 1. After Class, Write Test-Review Notes: Association Cues

1. Right after class, read your class notes, and condense them into Test Review Notes ✔

2. Choose a study area that is free of external and social distractions ✔

3. Eat a Power Study Snack to stay energized and focused (see list) ✔

4. Manage your time ✔

    Estimate Time (Fantasy):   Start Time: Finish Time: Actual Time (Reality):

5. Do the facts need further clarification (see textbook, tutoring center, or teacher)? ✔

6. To ace your test, use Association Cues to memorize the facts for Instant and Total Recall ✔

Write Memory Association Cues for Instant and Total Recall
(Use pencil to change a cue that doesn't work)

Part 2. After Class, Write Test Review Notes: Create Test Questions

7. Visualize the test questions. Convert the facts into test questions: Who? Why? Where? What? ✔

8. Self-Test for strengths and weaknesses. Change the weak memory cues ✔

9. To ace your test: Review, Repetition, Retention, Recognition, and Instant and Total Recall ✔

Write Test Questions: Who, What? Where? When? Why?

My Class Notes   Date:

Topic:

Write down the <u>Main Idea</u> and the supporting <u>Details</u>, <u>Examples</u>, or <u>Arguments</u>:

_____
_____
_____
_____
_____
_____
_____
_____
_____
_____
_____
_____
_____
_____
_____
_____
_____
_____
_____
_____
_____
_____
_____
_____
_____
_____
_____
_____
_____
_____
_____
_____
_____
_____
_____
_____

Part 1. After Class, Write Test-Review Notes: Association Cues

1. Right after class, read your class notes, and condense them into Test Review Notes ✔

2. Choose a study area that is free of external and social distractions ✔

3. Eat a Power Study Snack to stay energized and focused (see list) ✔

4. Manage your time ✔

   Estimate Time (Fantasy):   Start Time: Finish Time: Actual Time (Reality):

5. Do the facts need further clarification (see textbook, tutoring center, or teacher)? ✔

6. To ace your test, use Association Cues to memorize the facts for Instant and Total Recall ✔

Write Memory Association Cues for Instant and Total Recall
(Use pencil to change a cue that doesn't work)

Part 2. After Class, Write Test Review Notes: Create Test Questions

7. Visualize the test questions. Convert the facts into test questions: Who? Why? Where? What? ✔

8. Self-Test for strengths and weaknesses. Change the weak memory cues ✔

9. To ace your test: Review, Repetition, Retention, Recognition, and Instant and Total Recall ✔

Write Test Questions: Who, What? Where? When? Why?

My Class Notes   Date:

Topic:

Write down the <u>Main Idea</u> and the supporting <u>Details</u>, <u>Examples</u>, or <u>Arguments</u>:

_____
_____
_____
_____
_____
_____
_____
_____
_____
_____
_____
_____
_____
_____
_____
_____
_____
_____
_____
_____
_____
_____
_____
_____
_____
_____
_____
_____
_____
_____
_____

My Class Notes Continued . . .

Part 1. After Class, Write Test-Review Notes: Association Cues

1. Right after class, read your class notes, and condense them into Test Review Notes ✔
2. Choose a study area that is free of external and social distractions ✔
3. Eat a Power Study Snack to stay energized and focused (see list) ✔
4. Manage your time ✔

   Estimate Time (Fantasy):   Start Time: Finish Time: Actual Time (Reality):

5. Do the facts need further clarification (see textbook, tutoring center, or teacher)? ✔
6. To ace your test, use Association Cues to memorize the facts for Instant and Total Recall ✔

Write Memory Association Cues for Instant and Total Recall
(Use pencil to change a cue that doesn't work)

Part 2. After Class, Write Test Review Notes: Create Test Questions

7. Visualize the test questions. Convert the facts into test questions: Who? Why? Where? What? ✔

8. Self-Test for strengths and weaknesses. Change the weak memory cues ✔

9. To ace your test: Review, Repetition, Retention, Recognition, and Instant and Total Recall ✔

Write Test Questions: Who, What? Where? When? Why?

My Class Notes   Date:

Topic:

Write down the <u>Main Idea</u> and the supporting <u>Details</u>, <u>Examples</u>, or <u>Arguments</u>:

_____
_____
_____
_____
_____
_____
_____
_____
_____
_____
_____
_____
_____
_____
_____
_____
_____
_____
_____
_____
_____
_____
_____
_____
_____
_____
_____
_____
_____
_____
_____
_____

Part 1. After Class, Write Test-Review Notes: Association Cues

1. Right after class, read your class notes, and condense them into Test Review Notes ✔

2. Choose a study area that is free of external and social distractions ✔

3. Eat a Power Study Snack to stay energized and focused (see list) ✔

4. Manage your time ✔

    Estimate Time (Fantasy):   Start Time: Finish Time: Actual Time (Reality):

5. Do the facts need further clarification (see textbook, tutoring center, or teacher)? ✔

6. To ace your test, use Association Cues to memorize the facts for Instant and Total Recall ✔

Write Memory Association Cues for Instant and Total Recall
(Use pencil to change a cue that doesn't work)

Part 2. After Class, Write Test Review Notes: Create Test Questions

7. Visualize the test questions. Convert the facts into test questions: Who? Why? Where? What? ✔

8. Self-Test for strengths and weaknesses. Change the weak memory cues ✔

9. To ace your test: Review, Repetition, Retention, Recognition, and Instant and Total Recall ✔

Write Test Questions: Who, What? Where? When? Why?

My Class Notes

Date:

Topic:

Write down the <u>Main Idea</u> and the supporting <u>Details</u>, <u>Examples</u>, or <u>Arguments</u>:

_____
_____
_____
_____
_____
_____
_____
_____
_____
_____
_____
_____
_____
_____
_____
_____
_____
_____
_____
_____
_____
_____
_____
_____
_____
_____
_____
_____
_____
_____
_____
_____
_____
_____
_____

Part 1. After Class, Write Test-Review Notes: Association Cues

1. Right after class, read your class notes, and condense them into Test Review Notes ✔
2. Choose a study area that is free of external and social distractions ✔
3. Eat a Power Study Snack to stay energized and focused (see list) ✔
4. Manage your time ✔

   Estimate Time (Fantasy):   Start Time: Finish Time: Actual Time (Reality):

5. Do the facts need further clarification (see textbook, tutoring center, or teacher)? ✔
6. To ace your test, use Association Cues to memorize the facts for Instant and Total Recall ✔

Write Memory Association Cues for Instant and Total Recall
(Use pencil to change a cue that doesn't work)

Part 1. After Class, Write Test-Review Notes: Association Cues

Part 2. After Class, Write Test Review Notes: Create Test Questions

7. Visualize the test questions. Convert the facts into test questions: Who? Why? Where? What? ✔

8. Self-Test for strengths and weaknesses. Change the weak memory cues ✔

9. To ace your test: Review, Repetition, Retention, Recognition, and Instant and Total Recall ✔

Write Test Questions: Who, What? Where? When? Why?

My Class Notes   Date:

Topic:

Write down the <u>Main Idea</u> and the supporting <u>Details</u>, <u>Examples</u>, or <u>Arguments</u>:

_____
_____
_____
_____
_____
_____
_____
_____
_____
_____
_____
_____
_____
_____
_____
_____
_____
_____
_____
_____
_____
_____
_____
_____
_____
_____
_____
_____
_____
_____
_____

Part 1. After Class, Write Test-Review Notes: Association Cues

1. Right after class, read your class notes, and condense them into Test Review Notes ✔

2. Choose a study area that is free of external and social distractions ✔

3. Eat a Power Study Snack to stay energized and focused (see list) ✔

4. Manage your time ✔

      Estimate Time (Fantasy):   Start Time: Finish Time: Actual Time (Reality):

5. Do the facts need further clarification (see textbook, tutoring center, or teacher)? ✔

6. To ace your test, use Association Cues to memorize the facts for Instant and Total Recall ✔

Write Memory Association Cues for Instant and Total Recall
(Use pencil to change a cue that doesn't work)

Part 2. After Class, Write Test Review Notes: Create Test Questions

7. Visualize the test questions. Convert the facts into test questions: Who? Why? Where? What? ✔

8. Self-Test for strengths and weaknesses. Change the weak memory cues ✔

9. To ace your test: Review, Repetition, Retention, Recognition, and Instant and Total Recall ✔

Write Test Questions: Who, What? Where? When? Why?

Our Power Study Snack Suggestions

Choose One of Our Power Study Snacks or Create Your Own Energy Menu

1. **Nutritious Pizza**
   Whole Wheat Pita, Mozzarella Cheese Slice, Tomato Slice, Basil Leaf, and Olive Oil, Microwave 30 Seconds

2. **Humus and Veggies**
   Carrots, Celery, Broccoli, Red Peppers . . .

3. **Bran Muffin**
   Apple-Oat, Cranberry-Walnut, Banana-Pecan . . .

4. **Sports Bar with 10+ Grams of Protein**
   Avoid High Amounts of Saturated Fat or Hydrogenated Vegetable Oils

5. **A Small 3oz. Can of Tuna/Sardines with 4-6 Whole Grain Crackers**

6. **One Container of Low Fat Yogurt Sprinkled with High Fiber Cereal and Fresh Fruit**

7. **Whole-Grain Cereal with Fat Free or 1% Low Fat Milk and Fresh Fruit**

8. **Trail Mix: Your Favorite Nuts**
   Peanuts, Almonds, Cashews, Pistachios with Raisins and Cranberries . . .

9. **Dried Fruit Mix: Your Favorite Fruits**
   Apricots, Pineapple, Apple Chips, Banana Chips . . .

10. **Vegetable Soup and a Slice of Whole Grain Bread**

11. **Chocolate Smoothie: Chocolate Soy Milk, Peanut Butter, and Whey Protein**

12. **Oatmeal-Raisin Cookie**

My Power Study Snacks

List Your Favorite Power Study Snacks to Stay Energized and Focused

1. _____

2. _____

3. _____

4. _____

5. _____

6. _____

7. _____

8. _____

9. _____

10. _____

PHOTON
SUPERHERO of EDUCATION ®

EVERY DAY AN EASY A

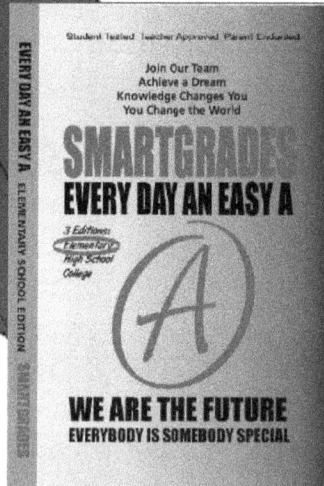

Student Tested Teacher Approved Parent Endorsed

Join Our Team
Achieve a Dream
Knowledge Changes You
You Change the World

SMARTGRADES
EVERY DAY AN EASY A

3 Editions:
Elementary
High School
College

WE ARE THE FUTURE
EVERYBODY IS SOMEBODY SPECIAL

EVERY DAY AN EASY A ELEMENTARY SCHOOL EDITION SMARTGRADES

EVERY DAY AN EASY A
3 Editions: Elementary, High School, College
ACE EVERY TEST EVERY TIME
All Global Bookstores

www.BooksNotBombs.com
EVERYBODY IS SOMEBODY SPECIAL

---

1 Minute Time Management Class
10 Steps to Success
EVERY DAY AN EASY A ©All Rights Reserved, 2010.

Step 1 ☐
Make a Daily Action Plan
Write Down Your Big Goals

Step 2 ☐
Set Your Priorities
Urgent, Important, Low, and Optional

Step 3 ☐
Breakdown Your Dreams
Breakdown Big Goal into Smaller Steps
List Steps Necessary to Complete Big Goal

Step 4 ☐
Divide and Conquer
Take Baby Steps Toward Reaching Goal
Crawl. Walk. Fly. Soar...

Step 5 ☐
Use Time Logs: Estimated Vs. Actual Time
e.g., Estimate Time for Lunch: 1 Hour
Actual Time: 20 Minutes
40 Minutes for Errands: Bank, Post Office, Store

Step 6 ☐
Life Is a Bumpy Road
Make Time for Delays, Detours,
Distractions, and Disappointments
e.g., Copier Runs Out of Toner and Paper

Step 7 ☐
Use Checkboxes to Keep Track of Completed Tasks

Step 8 ☐
Review and Refine Daily Action Plan
Pay Attention to Strengths and Weaknesses

Step 9 ☐
Celebrate Your Success
Celebrate Job Well Done with Daily Reward

Step 10 ☐
EVERY DAY AN EASY A
www.everydayaneasya.com

PHOTON
EVERY DAY AN EASY A

Dark Ages Despair.
PHOTON Is Here.

Enlightenment Is Her Destiny.
World Peace Is Her Legacy.

Nurture the Human Brain.
Keep Planet Earth Sane.

Ignorance Is the Enemy.
Education Is the Remedy.

SMARTGRADES
SCHOOL NOTEBOOKS
Will Prevail.
No Student Will Fail.

Students and Educators Are a Team.
Good Grades Become Grand Dreams.

Ignorance Is Bitter Not Bliss.
I Seal this Promise with a Kiss.

BUY NOW!
AMAZON 2 DAY SHIP
GLOBAL BOOKSTORES

EVERY DAY AN EASY A
TOTAL RECALL
YOUR STUDY ROOM IS UNDER NEW MANAGEMENT
SMARTGRADES SCHOOL NOTEBOOKS AND ACADEMIC PLANNER

EVERYBODY IS SOMEBODY SPECIAL
www.BooksNotBombs.com

Student Tested Teacher Approved Parent Endorsed
Join Our Team
Achieve a Dream
Knowledge Changes You
You Change the World
SMARTGRADES
EVERY DAY AN EASY A
3 Edition:
Elementary
High School
College
WE ARE THE FUTURE
EVERYBODY IS SOMEBODY SPECIAL
EVERY DAY AN EASY A · ELEMENTARY SCHOOL EDITION

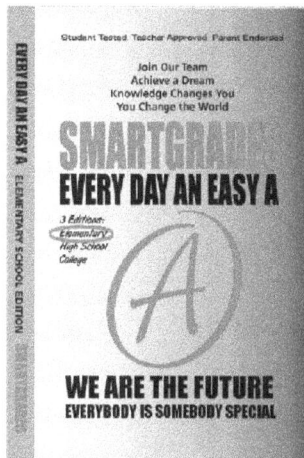

www.ingramcontent.com/pod-product-compliance
Lightning Source LLC
Chambersburg PA
CBHW081154090426

42736CB00017B/3326

9 781885 872654